waterways books

Travelling East
by Road and Soul

releasing new voices, revealing new perspectives

Travelling East by Road and Soul

waterways
www.waterways-publishing.com
an imprint of flipped eye publishing

First Edition
Copyright © Camilla Reeve, 2009
Cover Image © Camilla Reeve, 2009
Cover Design © Petraski, flipped eye publishing, 2009

All Rights Reserved. No part of this publication may be reproduced, stored in a retrieval system, or transmitted, in any form, or by any means, electronic, mechanical, photocopying, recording or otherwise, without prior consent.

ISBN-10: 1-905233-22-1
ISBN-13: 978-1-905233-22-9

British Library Cataloguing in Publication Data
A catalogue record for this book is available from the British Library

Editorial work for this book was supported by the Arts Council of England

Printed and Bound in the United Kingdom

LOTTERY FUNDED

Travelling East
by Road and Soul

Camilla Reeve
2009

Travelling East by Road and Soul

Soul-dark Breakwaters	7
Beggars Belief	**8**
Taking Friends to the Airport	10
Olives in the Hand	**12**
The Beaten Zone	13
City at 6 a.m	**14**
European Secrets	16
House in Kosovo	**17**
Knock at the Door	18
Dark Bird Turning	**19**
Koukounaries Lagoon	20
Lalaria Beach	**21**
Taking the Bus	22
Waiting for a Wall	**24**
Moments	25
Fatima's Pattern	**26**
The Red Rose Seller	28
Time to Play With	**29**
Hour of Prayer	30
Transition	**32**
Home at Nakapiripirit Camp	33
First Lesson in Mindli Town	**34**
Death-mates at Khafji	35
Village of Death	**38**
Winter Angels	40
The Gap Between Them	**42**
Grand Ledges	44
Possibilities	**46**
No shaman	47
Ivy Man	**48**
The Meaning of Beads	49
Toumani Diabaté Playing the Kora	**50**
Bird Sanctuary Volunteer	52
Going to meet the Vole Man	**53**
A Moment Together	55

London, England: 0°

Soul-dark Breakwaters

No way to stop the tide from flowing –

from surging in the Autumn,
up
shingle, up and over the lowest slick
struts
of soul-dark breakwaters –

no way to stop you going.

And I know it so I never try,

not wanting you to feel resentment
or know
how sad your leaving makes me
or go
from here without my blessing

to where you can't help wanting to be gone.

Beggars Belief

A woman and a boy come begging at my door,
sheltering in my porch from the rain,
"Refugees from Kosovo," says their cardboard.

Money for her and a tangerine for him
but she insists I give him money too
so I come through with it.

*In the filmed review of nineteen ninety-nine,
a grandmother was riding up the mountain side
on a donkey's back, fleeing from the Serbs,
arthritic fingers slipping on the icy harness.*

Another one approaches with a sleeping toddler
draped across a shoulder. I give her money
and an anorak.

*If I give this beggar the money that I'm holding
it can't help the grandmother on the donkey's back;
but does that matter?*

*If this beggar woman is not from Kosovo
but a Gypsy maybe or from somewhere else,
should that bother me?*

Then a third one with a baby and some cardboard.
Money almost gone and temper shredded,
I lock my door.

Now she's out there pleading through the door-jamb
and I'm in here trying to ignore her,
feeling awful.

The fleeing grandmother and her ageing donkey
sway slowly up the hill, away from everything they know
except for life.

Taking Friends to the Airport

Sleep drugs me,
knocking at the door,
murmur *Yes*,
roll off mattress
into clothes, shoes,
grab keys, glasses,
load friends, cases,
drive to motorway,
insert car into traffic stream,
dream
of flying sheep,
try not to sleep,
wonder if we'll be on time . . .

finally we make it,
unload friends, cases,
exchange hugs, kisses,
email addresses,
alone then,
drive home again,
unlock door, undress,
unmake everything,
insert body into bed sheets,
try to relax,
fail to fall asleep . . .

wonder if they're really on their way to Mexico
or has it been a dream?
Remember wondering if we would be on time.

Ah!
Settle properly to sleep.
Don't believe in much these days
but always believe in my wonderings.

Palma de Mallorca, Spain: 2.65°

Olives in the Hand

A day so hot that olives laid around a dish
were almost sweet against the tongue beneath the shade.

A man passed by. The woman saw but wouldn't look.
The bread was rough, the olives raw, she had no need.

A day so hot that date-palms groaned unharvested,
yearning for when the sun would sink below the waves.

The man came back but she resisted his appeal,
preferring olives in the hand to ones on the tree.

Ypres, Belgium: 2.88°

The Beaten Zone

The beaten zone still shows its cratered bruises
where machine-guns ate into the ground.

From Poperinghe right up to Hooge
each route is edged with pools
where shells aimed at the road fell short or long
and soldiers died who'd otherwise have lived
at least another day of carnage.

A land so scarred by mortar, shell and trench
that even now, when almost all
the men have found their friends in death,
its brokenness appals,

opens for me a view onto the instant
of their falling, their drawn-out torment,
a wound in Time that will not heal
or let itself be closed.

Hamburg, Germany: 10.00°

City at 6 a.m

At dawn the city yawns – gigantic metal jaws,
trawls for a tithe of everybody's labour,
their sweat and hopes and lives.

Thumping insistent chant of two trains passing,
all lights illuminated, one train entering the station
one moving out of sight.

Full train seen through steamy station windows,
bright as a live volcano. Business-like
bustling erupts – these travellers have rights.

Along the streets in shop and office doorways,
hiding from weather and police raids,
guest workers finish up their night.

Passing by them, dances of cars play
follow-my-leader, big headlights disclosing
metre on cobbled metre of carefully woven stripes.

Snow-blown concentric circles form heart-shapes
with canals that over history have drained, from many
hinterlands, the city's business life:

long barges filled with corn, iron bars, timber
and stone, old tributes taken and gone. The city
swallows people now rather than metal pipes.

On the canal, red and white puddled lights radiate
and bridges frame them. Swallowing people
is no accident, not in this vista thought through

for the burger-masters' personal delight.

Vienna, Austria: 16.37°

European Secrets

Through my plane window, I glimpse mountains.
They march below me for an hour,
profiles stern, dignified, both dark and bright.
Here fresh snow wept, there wind left marks,
steel-scouring the heights, leaving their faces scarred,
abrupt, sculpted by age, as mine might seem to children
who don't know me – a thing apart,
not to be touched or tangled with.

A glacier, immeasurably slow, creeps between two ridges,
drawn down by weight and the corrosive toll of years.
Its whitish-yellow surface speaks of European secrets
that, at fifty-eight, maybe I'm not yet old enough to know –
the ones our parents whispered behind bedroom doors.
Peering deep into a crevasse, I seem to hear it crackle
and sense the walls of past lives closing in on me –
the icy grip of history that robbed them all
of easy nights curled up with love and days of joy.

Then we fly on as new snow veils the old;
nature excelling at masking traces of the past.
The engines hum, the hostess' trolley coasts along the aisle,
I lean my head against the airline seat and doze,
our history forgotten for a while.

See Endnote 1

Pristina, Kosovo: 21.15°

House in Kosovo

Black oak door swinging in the wind,
you don't need to go and close it.
Red tiles loose, slipping from the roof,
may no-one try to set them straight.
Let the rain come, let it fall right in.

More than seventy outside my window,
piled up, like potatoes, under sacks.
Piled up roughly but don't you worry –
bodies aren't needed on that journey.

More than seventy women and children,
riddled with bullet-holes, torn
and broken. Never again will
that old door
lead to my home. Leave the roof unfixed,
let my tears fall in.

See Endnote 2

Knock at the Door

Is that them coming for you now?
Unlooked-for noises from the street:
a lorry's rumbling tread;
doors banging; the tramp of feet on stairs.
I am consumed by dread –
they may be coming soon.

Somehow, I'm in last year again
with its sudden night-time purges.
Scared, close to swooning
and overcome with sweats,
I fold and refold your jacket and press
knife-pleated creases in your trousers.

Dark Bird Turning

What news flies on the wings of a dark bird,
midnight blue, over a stranger's roof?
No news, brother,
except the tale you tell
within your secret heart
when friend or child are late.

What luck hangs
from the claws of a vulture seen,
turning and turning
over a foreign town?
No luck, sister,
but the kind that we are born with
which now is wearing thin.

No news brother,
but my pain at your suffering,
no luck sister
but my wish that we both survive.

Skiathos, Greece: 23.48°

Koukounaries Lagoon

Finely tuned in time and space,
the counterclaims of rival cicadas
keep fluctuating, repeating
a prehistoric soundscape.

Parched lilac herbs beside the lake
are the exclusive preserve of butterflies
whose powder-blue and lime-green
wings show mauve when feeding.

The tribe of fish that surfaces
to breathe on burning days
through concave lenses gazes uncomprehending
at curving pines and overhanging reeds.

For now, at least, the balance holds
between them, they are sustained.

Lalaria Beach

Lalaria:
Rainbow waters.

Aeons:
Snow-white marble
veined with gold.

Millennia
formed the cliff,
layer on layer,
saw it lift.

Centuries
weathered the stack,
dug fissures deep,
heard them crack,
thunder to the beach.

Seasons:
Storms from the North
hammered the stones,
rendered them smooth,
pallid as bone,
polished jewels.

Just an hour
in which the tourists visit
and through seawater
see the sunlight

casting rainbows;
love the vision,
steal the stones.

Lalaria.
Rhythm echoes on.

Taking the Bus

The tourist guide tells us:
On Skiathos, the buses
are excellent value
with doors on hydraulic
and blinds at each window . . .

But they're
bouncing and noisy
and drowning in people,
while scouring the hillsides
for more willing victims,

who've stood for so long
with the heat beating down,
that they're desperate to board
and to hell with the schedule,
but, all the same, nervous
they'll never escape –

as the bus makes a bow-wave
when passing a car
or the lone zooming moped
of those braver-hearted,

who'd rather be windswept
and harried on bends
than crushed in a bus
till the absolute end
of its route.

Athens, Greece: 23.73°

Waiting for a Wall

Beside Piraeus harbour
piled up stones
have waited
more than three millennia
to be made into a wall.
Local masons

complain
the stones are incompatible
having come from all over,
but the captain's ghost
refuses to accept that,
his men having humped their load

sweating to this place –
a hundred weight of stone –
that was the order
they faithfully delivered on.
Nobody warned him
of the nationality of rocks

or said they had to share
a mother tongue.

Side, Turkey: 31.38°

Moments

The cat sits on the wall,
brindled fur merging with shadows imperceptibly.
Behind her, morning glory blossoms live their blue day
while dying purple ones sink into shade.

The cat sleeps.

A woman watches, motionless.
Primeval, slender, a lizard scuttles along the wall.
Grey scales blending with sun-baked stone,
he hunts.

The woman breathes out once.
She's waited months
for such a moment.
The lizard darts and gulps;
a fly's life ends;
alerted by movement, the cat hurtles
after the lizard,
which escapes.
The cat
subsides again, waiting for its moment.

The woman smiles.

Fatima's Pattern

This holiday, they walk me round the pool.
They are all gentle, loving and attentive;
I am diffident, accepting, courteous.
I never asked to have them lead me by the hand,
to be stone-blind, to be their unwed sister.
I never asked for any of these things.
But nor did they.

The moon, they say, is far too full,
she has disturbed the tides,
it would be foolish, for a girl like me,
to think of swimming from the beach.
I know the feeling of 'too full'
after the kind of meal when everyone
has taken turns to feed me.

My brother says some birds flew overhead.
I didn't hear their cries
as I might do in my own garden.
I listen, hope for a sound I'll recognise,
to form a link between this far-off place
and where I live – my usual pattern –
but I hear nothing.

One day my darlings all go out at once.
At last, alone, the peace sinks into me.
A single bird cheeps softly, tucked into a bush;
with no-one talking in my ear, I hear it.
The hotel pool splashes and gurgles
as someone swims a length, I can do that.

Reaching out, I find the foreign door catch
and turn it well; there must be no mistakes.
With toes that seek the edges of each slab
and hands that creep along the fence and hedges,
I keep on going until I'm standing tall
just where the pool can lap around my feet.
The ground is wet, my soles grow chill.
I cannot feel the sun on head and arms.
Are you up there waiting yet, my sister moon?

In the distance I hear my brother call.
His tone is cautious but his footsteps hasten.
I practice standing calm and balanced,
savour the sense of poise and confidence,
this is the pattern that I wish to follow
whatever any of them say or do.
Must I still wait for every morsel
that other hands will place into my mouth?

Sister moon, my unseen friend
who can't help being too full, blind-sided, stared at,
who never asked to circumnavigate the globe
or have some vast symbolic role,
are you too far away to see the tears I cry
or hear them splash their last into the pool?

The Red Rose Seller

He bears red roses in a plastic bucket,
far more than even he could hope to sell
–though hope must be his most enduring asset –
if all the women on the beach were beautiful
and all the men romantic.

But why bring such a vast array of flowers?
Is it because he has nowhere to lay them,
no cool and constant place for going back to,
neither a shack, like waiters paid to chase him,
nor three-star hotel room like ours?

We say "no" several times with courtesy
yet still he presses us to buy a rose,
Your daughter wants one, says his knowing nod.
At last, brave smile and ramrod back, he goes,
taking with him my certainty.

I wonder why I constantly avoid this,
ignore the look of hope upon his face
– when hope and roses could be all he has;
maybe I'm just too middle-aged and English;
exposed to pressure, I resist.

By the third night, our last one here, he knows
there's no point in persisting with our party.
He gives our restaurant table a wide berth,
leaving me drained, regretful,
and painfully aware of hope and roses.

Time to Play With

The red rose seller trudges past, arms empty,
his jaw relaxed at last from hopeful grins.
Too early to be trading flowers with tourists
so he has time to play with.

Up in the campsite on the drifting dunes
someone is fooling with a little drum,
picking out rhythms from North Africa,
the Asian Steppes and London.

Perhaps the drummer's twin lived here before,
making Mark Antony and Cleopatra pause
to wonder where the distant music came from
before they shared their world-transforming kiss?

It is the Year of European Union,
the hour when shade still cools the ancient sand,
the moment when a single leaf's descent
rings louder than the evening that will come.

Two people whisper underneath my balcony –
a man and woman, low and passionate.
Are they descended from some great ones,
are *all* of us inheritors?

Behind their murmurs sound the lapping waves
as softly-spoken and drawn-out as tender greetings –
Inshallah – washing the beach so its blank canvas
can be imprinted by each person's footprints.

The year, the hour, the moment balance here
and I have time to play with too.

See Endnote 3

Sharm-el-Sheikh, Egypt: 34.17°

Hour of Prayer

One man walks towards the mosque,
hem of white robes flapping against sandals,
hands swinging loosely at his sides;
face serene, remote, focused on the minaret
and the holy message coming from its spire.

Later, three friends walk towards the mosque,
each man hurried and unspeaking,
arms flexing slightly as if he'd break into a run
were it not undignified;
the hour grows nearer, time presses on them.

A lone man struggles to fill a borrowed taxi
with massive sacks of rubble,
working against the clock,
but the muezzin grows ever more insistent.
Ruefully locking the taxi, he goes to worship

leaving behind a street that's almost motionless:
just one cat arching its back and leaping up walls
to scan for rats, two dogs sniffing the taxi,
fascinated by the sewage scent of rubble,
and stray bougainvillea bracts,
torn by wind from the mother plant,
blowing along the pavement,
their slender violet profiles
vulnerable against the steel-grey tarmac.

Now the muezzin has fallen silent,
the hour of prayer is passing,
I ask myself, in all this public sharing
of devotion,
was there an element I missed?

Transition

At the moment of transition from air to water,
from wearing my snorkel but knowing I'm not submerged
to letting nose and mouth and ears sink under,
I'm never more aware of my two selves:

the believing self that loves to greet the fish,
that thrills to coral, trips out on light through ripples
in a drifty dreamy place where I slip back
to when the world I sensed was interlinked –

all creatures, water, rocks and air – to me;
and the cautious doubting self that hesitates,
seeks logic, explanations, certainty,
feels water round my ears and starts to panic,

finds every reason why I should stay safe.
Fish-like, I writhe in a net of their contriving,
my two selves tangled on the shore of strife
until my face breaks through the surface and I see under sea.

See Endnote 4

Nakapiripirit, Uganda: 34.78°

Home at Nakapiripirit Camp

At the end of the path from the well,
at the end of the track from the road,
at the end of the walk from the Sudan,
at the end of years of struggle for her beliefs,
and of being driven out and away
someone has made a home.

In the middle of the day,
in the middle of the refugee camp,
of the group of camps;
in the middle of a country edged by war;
in the middle of a continent
stands a round mud hut.

And written around its walls
in letters of blood and ash,
in letters of fear conquered,
in letters the width of a hand are these words:
Man ot pa Regina –

This is Regina's hut.

See Endnote 5

Mindli, Diyala Province, Iraq: 44.55°

First Lesson in Mindli Town

They walked to school that morning,
history homework and protractors safely strapped in rucksacks.
Each had a different lunch from mother, aunt or older sister –
falafel, two tangerines, ripe dates, some cheese and onion crisps –
maybe they'd eat together by the tree in the school courtyard,
maybe one would have eaten his or hers before lunch started.
Who knows what children will do?

They walked to school that morning,
threading through army checkpoints in walled-off districts,
keen to reach the school's main door, be off the streets,
even if unready for tests or having tiffs with their best friends;
and gratefully they made it, left shoes in racks, rucksacks on pegs,
knelt for morning prayers and sat at desks for register.

Then the airstrike came.

They walked to school that morning, yet
ten won't be walking back, seven won't walk anywhere again.
We laid out bodies side by side, those recognisable as children,
a desperate geometry. For the rest, we counted body parts
to check we had them all, one final test of our arithmetic.
Then we wrapped our lost ones to keep them warm
in the over-long hereafter, veiled their faces
because we loved them too much to leave them.

See Endnote 6

Ras al Khafji, Kuwait: 48.52°

Death-mates at Khafji

Side by side the bodies stretch
across the sand
as lovers,
one with his hand
upon the other's,
faces turned each to each
and yet, not
a new
Romeo and Juliet
but two young men.

On my left is one who died
to take
some land
that wasn't his,
to help
some people
he had never met,
part of a war
defined as being just,
for country,
God and peace.
His death-mate died
to hold
some land
that wasn't his,
to hurt
some people
who had hurt his friends,
for God and country

See Endnote 7

yet so much wishing
to fly home again in peace.

They could be kin, skin dark,
hair
curled as twins,
one seems to smile
and one died shouting.
I mourn the lack
of who they might have been.

Only
respect –
I have to grant them that.

Their weapons gone,
the various shades of cloth
are all that show
which side
they fought for.
Grey, fawn and brown,
meant to blend in with rock,
were not enough
to keep them safe that day.

There is no camouflage
when morning comes.
Stark light picks out
the labels on right feet,
the numbers in a log,
waiting for body bags –
one black,

one red –
to carry them away.

They might be brothers
maybe even friends.
Perhaps,
some day,
their sons will be.
For these two here,
mated in death,
whatever I may dream,
their day is spent.

My Lai, Vietnam: 108.87°

Village of Death

Into my village of death
came not just one
but ninety men
with their guns cocked

and their flies open.

What they did then,
what they have done,
is something for which
there were no words.

Yet words must be

invented and spoken,
used as a warning,
so that this thing,
this dreadful act,
need never happen

to a place again.

The ditch was full that Spring
full up
with bodies –
tiny and large and thin

all broken up and red,

full of murmurs too
and of stifled sighs,
no louder noises
than pain may force
between the frightened
lips

of wounded,

no more noise
now
that all the dying
have their business done.

See Endnote 8

Bohai Gulf, China: 118.57°

Winter Angels

Every year my village
welcomes migrating swans as if we honoured ancestors,
calls them our winter angels.

They come to feast on seaweed fringes
encumbering the kelp nets that criss-cross our bay
and leave the ropes pecked clean for next year's crop;

Their brave, white, far-flying beauty of form and spirit
brings luck and honour. We share with them
unleavened bread, our children's voices, happiness.

But this winter I, who am, who have not –
for one whole year – felt, after what happened,
really myself, wish to be gone. Away from here,

not spilling sadness
out of my kelp net and into others, walk to the headland,
weeks before the angels' anticipated landfall;

the rasping netted sorrows drag there after me,
forcing tears through shuttered eyes, rusting my cheeks,
leaving me weaker even than before and all alone,

and then

a curdling of the light,
as cockles dimple damp tidal sand with secret pinholes of their breath,
something coming but too far off and far too soon for certain.

Hope surges painfully from chest to throat.

First, shapes appear against the sun. Then suddenly they're settling all round me.
At long last here, their coming puts final flight to older thoughts.

I hold my arms out wide, they spread their wings.
Slowly we dance together, rising and falling, greeting each other as this year's winter angels.

See Endnote 9

Traverse City, Michigan, USA: -85.59°

The Gap Between Them

They walk,
mother and grown-up son,
snow gone at last, on sand.
How few days till they part?
She wants
to touch his hand,
would do so with her daughters,
restricts herself to leaning on his arm
then lets him go again. Again.

Bayshore,
scraped icy-raw by wind,
no shelter here from Arctic storms.
Austere.
A giving-no-quarter land,
stripped down to fundamentals,
functional, resolute, plain,
unsoftened but for the
light buff fuzz of last year's reeds.

She wonders
what else is there to say?
This is his place now, this
vast, seasonally-glaciated, chunk of the world's surface
spreading east and north and west so very far
yet never far as her.

Any remark
might be perceived as critical
of his decision, or simply desperation.

Yet saying nothing
under the arch of such a teal-blue sky
flashed back from lake and beach-wide pools;
such sticky buds,
wind-driven sideways and about to burst,
seems like being surly.

She photographs the bay,
the reeds, the buds,
shares the photo with him,
feels less alone.

Grand Ledge, Michigan, USA: -84.72°

Grand Ledges

She had told him of Grand Ledges, how she yearned
to see their beauty, feel their age,
be at the centre of the earth on this journey of journeys.
So he said he'd take her there, the one he turned to
and protected, lay beside at night and laughed with.

The going was hard.
His map was incomplete, unclear,
yet he knew the direction;
kept heading south-west by the sun
till they reached Grand River and the ancient place
where maple syrup runs clear
at the turning of the leaf,
where mountains fold themselves into ledges
fine as woven belt-thongs; where they sink deep
into the earth as the lair
a mother bear hollows for her cubs;
where mountains have been folding
and sinking since before the first tale told.

When they scrambled down into the
silence of the woods
a squirrel scampered away through ferns
and a bluejay shrieked its warning.
He waited for her
to acknowledge their safe arrival at her goal.
Instead she spoke of the folds
not being as deep as she had hoped
and the wind much colder than she wanted.

Quietly he agreed it was late in the season –
already swallows gathered in high places,
practising before their journey south,
small dark forms flickering against the sky's brightness
as shoals of salmon-fry
at their first taste of the sea's vast salty mouth.

Then they crossed a narrow bridge above the creek
and his hand steadied her,
warm as the south wind that she missed.
His kisses came sweet
as maple syrup beading on dark trunks,
his eyes shone grey as the sky's light on the river,
where red and golden leaves
floated in their hundreds,
waiting to be clasped by the grip of winter
and swept away in the unruly floods of spring.

He watched her scan the further bank
but did not hear her whisper:
What will help me remember today
among all the thoughts that sink
into the deep folds of my heart?

Then she saw light from red and golden leaves,
transmuted by water's gentle motion
into a radiant orange pool.
Two became one and she took that
as her key to memory.

See Endnote 10

Saginaw, Michigan, USA: -83.93°

Possibilities

Sister and brother trees,
whispers rustling at my window,
tell me some of what you know,
share with me.

We know when cold is coming.
Last night we went from green to amber –
our warning winter's near.

A short-lived spirit passing by,
at a distance your essence splits
into possibilities:

A cloud across the dawn,
an owl's brief theft of moonlight,
easy ambling shadows of deer and fawn
fearless at sunset?

Step closer. Let your breath
sweeten the air between our leaves,
bring back that legendary season
when we first saw ourselves in human dreams.

No shaman

The new moon's kayak
travels beside me on a sunset stream,
fire-bright, feather-light, fall-coloured,
into the falling of true night.

How can I be shaman to a people
who leave no room for Spirit,
or build a bridge for them to cross
that's rooted in the Spirit world but rootless here?

Approaching Saginaw,
our road turns west of south,
cutting the line of sight from me to moon,
leaving her kayak to glide the skies alone.

Valparaiso, Chile: -71.82°

Ivy Man

Against the stucco, swollen fronds
stretched
before struck loose by batons.
The loss of any single
stem
I might have borne
but the whole plant has gone.

Branching marks
show
where ivy was ripped away,
thrown
to its death, taking paint with it
into an early grave.

And no-one could save you.

After dark, shoulder-drenching
rain falls. I dream of you
reborn. Bags packed and ready to depart,
you go ahead of us –
as always –
riding a raft of thought.

See Endnote 11

Nouakchott, Mauritania: -15.58°

The Meaning of Beads

One bead at a time, she crafts them –
glass slurry and saliva, cast
overnight in salvaged sardine tins – then sells them;
kiffa beads that richer women
string together for their daughters,
colours sequenced by tradition
though sometimes she does wonder
what they mean:
   red-yellow-black-yellow-red-white-blue-white

At the market, dusty wind
from the wrong quarter veiling faces
cannot hide people's fear – is the Saharan
climate changing places?
Month on month, prices for bread and fish
climb higher and there is nothing she can do
but what she knows. So, one bead at a time,
she makes them:
   red-yellow-black-yellow-red-white-blue-white

In workshops with no air-conditioning,
a process that stains her skin,
throat more than once
too sore to talk, pay far too low but
safer than earned another way;
always she keeps the children's laughing faces
in her mind's eye, crafting their future
one bead at a time:
   red-yellow-black-yellow-red-white-blue-white

See Endnote 12

Bamako, Mali: -8.00°

Toumani Diabaté Playing the Kora

This man has listened.

He has heard rivers running
over sand and mud and stone,
has known of the rains' coming
before they came and felt the street's
steaming music after storm
in both his ears with his eyes
closed and a smile
of listening upon his lips.

He can stand still
with his fingers stilling
the kora strings,
ringed hands motionless
as a butterfly's wings
at the moment of rebirth,
and hear the rhythms hidden
in a single raindrop
before the earth
has time to drink it up.

He truly hears the river,
experiences its run
from source to delta.
Each pebble, grain of sand,
sliver of wood and stalk

made hollow by summer,
floating on, drifting in or rushed
over by the flood,
reach out to him as sounds.

Chords are his measure of time.
As water erodes a pebble into
sand, with every stroke
it makes the pebble hum a higher note
yet the bed of sand that mutes
the sound grows greater too, so
he never listens to one river twice
and hears it sing the same.

Nor can I listen as his kora plucks
the heartstrings in my chest,
teaching my ears and mind the path to hearing,
and not think back to the rivers of my past,
wishing Toumani could capture their music
for me.

See Endnote 13

Skomer Island, Wales: -5.00°

Bird Sanctuary Volunteer

At home my family will think about me,
follow my progress over Skomer Island.
With texts and maps and loving guesswork,
they'll try to tell where I will be each day,
what challenges I'll face, am I okay?
Two days might pass without hard news –
mobile reception here is poor at best –
but they'll stay hopeful.

And I – the one they focus on –
follow *your* progress
right along the coast,
word reaching me
from other birding sources: a visitor
who saw a mass of Manx
Shearwaters pass while he stood at St Anne's Head;
Guillemots are coming, claim researchers;
even I spot an offshore raft of Puffins.

On misty nights
I listen for your cries,
will I still be here when you all arrive?
Knowing the many dangers that you face
and torn
between a parent's anxious pride
and child's impatient urge
to see you fly,
I wait for you.

See Endnote 14

Going to meet the Vole Man

On my last morning and almost out
of 'Skomer' time, I raced
to meet him,
conscious of every second slipping by.

Dark in that wind-bleached land, moving away,
his blocky shoulders growing
more distant by the moment, I saw
the Skomer Vole Man.

So then I pressed on faster, my borrowed boots
biting into the path
and skidding pebbles down the slope, small thuds
that echoed my over-anxious heart.

At the site of his experiments
I saw long lines of stakes,
each marking a steel trap where, scenting food,
a vole will enter and find it can't escape.

Finding him, I faced the banter -
Where were you, lazybones,
at six a.m.? Sorry, I murmured,
unsure what lay beneath the joking.

Slipping broad fingers deep into a trap,
he prised out a tiny wriggling form -
This one's 'K3' and quite long-lived,
I tagged his ears last August.

Inching closer, I saw the vole was placid,
unfazed at being trapped.
Sure of its welcome, it snuggled in his hands,
let him caress its back.

They love being stroked, it's like
their mutual grooming.
When you've the right to work with wild creatures,
you must keep them happy and be good to them.

The gentling done, he slipped the drowsy vole
into a weighing sack,
Twenty-eight grams, then let it go. Watching him work,
my breathing eased, my hands relaxed.

Vole territories are ten metres square but see them as 3D,
the ground is full of tunnels.
Beneath my wary feet the mounded soil felt
fragile as an egg sucked out by gulls.

I thought of partnered voles lying safely underground,
grooming each other sleepily,
comparing ear-tags, watching their
tunnel roof bend in but never breach.

If they could talk like us, the male might say,
That'll be the Vole Man up there, love,
so don't you worry,
just one rare specimen and only found on Skomer.

A Moment Together

As I walked up from Skomer Head
to north-coast Garland Stone,
the sun was slowly setting.

Gulls perched on every nub of rock
and rabbits paused between the hillocks,
all of them facing sunwards
as if in worship.

For once the air was still –
each strand of fur and feather caught the glow
and lengthened shadows stretched out motionless.

Unnoticed, I looked my fill
at gull and rabbit as they beheld the sun.
Within my mind their images live on:
in moated island memories, I see them still.

-Endnotes

1	**Vienna,** situated on the Danube, feels culturally and geographically like part of Eastern Europe. Street signs point to easterly destinations like Budapest and Krakow; while the name "Danube" itself comes from the Iranian *dānu*, meaning "river".
2	**Pristina:** During the Kosovo Conflict's two separate wars, Pristina was at the centre of a vast displacement of people: 25% of the Kosovo population were forced out of their homes and, by June 1999, 433,300 Kosovan refugees were in Albania, 226,800 in Macedonia and 64,000 in Montenegro. Many returned but ethnic violence has flared up several times since, causing yet more deaths and displacement of people.
3	**Side** (pronounced *Seeday*) is supposed to be where Mark Antony met Queen Cleopatra.
4	**Sharm-el-Sheikh** is Egypt's main diving resort. In a region typified by sparsely populated arid environments, Sharm's focus is on protecting, and sharing with responsible tourists, the rich ecological variety lying just below the surface of the Red Sea.
5	**Nakapiripirit:** In 1969 I visited a refugee camp at Nakapiripirit as part of an Oxfam fact-finding mission. The camp was new, its Sudanese refugee inhabitants hopeful and full of energy. 40 years on, it's still there and other camps have sprung up around it. Children born in them from refugee parents are automatically defined as refugees. Many children also get killed in raids on the camps by a variety of Ugandan factions.
6	**Mindli Town** is situated in Diyala Province. On 08/05/2007, according to a Mindli Town policeman, a US helicopter was fired on from the ground and it hit the Al-Saada primary school with its return of fire, killing seven children and injuring three.

7	**Ras al Khafji** is the tiny coastal town a few kilometres from the Kuwait border where invading Iraqi forces first clashed with American, British and Kuwaiti troops. Many very young soldiers from both sides died on the beach.
8	**My Lai, Vietnam** (also called *Son My*) was a village of 700, mostly women and children, almost all of whom were killed by American troops in a search and destroy mission on 16/03/1968.
9	**Bohai Gulf, China** is the innermost gulf of the Yellow Sea and not far from Beijing. In the middle of one of the world's busiest and most polluted seaways lie coastal communities collecting shellfish, and cultivating kelp that they share with migrating swans, calling them "winter angels" (BBC - "Wild China - Tides of Change" July 2008)
10	**Grand Ledge** lies on the Grand River, which Native Americans called *O-wash-ta-nong* (Far-away-water) because of its length. 300-million-year-old sandstone and quartzite ledges rise 60 feet above the river's banks, creating a deep sense of protection and spirituality that, over the centuries, has drawn many groups to meditate and worship there.
11	**Valparaiso:** Many people were 'disappeared' by the Pinochet dictatorship during the 1970s. Legal cases about them are still going through the Chilean courts. In August 2008, for example, a judge ordered the arrest of 98 retired military and secret police officials in connection with the 1975 kidnapping of 42 dissidents.
12	**Nouakchott** is where the glass "Kiffa" beads come from that are sold in European accessory boutiques. Nouakchott was just a small fishing town till the North African drought of the 1970s caused a large influx of nomadic people. Its current population is over 2 million, many living in tented shanty towns in the desert around the city. Fresh water is scarce and food prices are spiralling. Now global warming is reversing the Saharan climate pattern, threatening further population displacement.

13	**Bamako** lies at the centre of the ancient African Kingdom of Mandé that created the *kora* (the 21-string harp). Kora music is performed by families of musicians known as *Jeliw,* or in French as *Griots*. Toumani Diabaté, world famous kora player and composer of the Mandé Varations, is descended from 53 generations of Griots from the Malinke tribe.
14	**Skomer Island** is a National Nature Reserve off the coast of Pembrokeshire. Half a million birds use the island during the summer including large breeding populations of Puffins, Razorbills, Guillemots, Fulmars and 40% of the world's Manx Shearwaters.

We Hope You Enjoyed Reading!
Let us know what you think by sending an e-mail to
editor@waterways-publishing.com

Thank You for buying *Travelling East by Road and Soul*. If you would like more information about waterways publishing, please join our mailing list online at **www.waterways-publishing.com**.

Visit our other imprints online:

mouthmark *(poetry)*
www.flippedeye.net/mouthmark

lubin & kleyner *(fiction)*
www.flippedeye.net/lubinandkleyner

flipped eye *(general)*
www.flippedeye.net